Whales

By Myrl Shireman
Illustrated By Pat St. Onge

COPYRIGHT © 2006 Mark Twain Media, Inc.

ISBN 1-58037-360-7

Printing No. D04109

Mark Twain Media, Inc., Publishers
Distributed by Carson-Dellosa Publishing Company, Inc.

Level 3: Book 1

Did you know there are many kinds of **whales**? The whale family is very large. The smallest whale is the dwarf sperm whale. It is only eight and one-half feet long. The largest whale is the blue whale, which is ninety-four feet long.

The picture to the right shows the size of a dwarf sperm whale when compared to the blue whale on the next page.

This is a close-up picture of a dwarf sperm whale.

Blue whale

Some whales feed by using their
baleen plates to strain food.

Some whales have teeth, but others have
baleen plates. The baleen plates are used to
filter the food the whale catches. One of the most
playful whales is the humpback whale. This whale
is larger than the dinosaurs that once lived on Earth.

One of the most famous whales is the sperm whale. The sperm whale was made famous in many books. Men went to sea on whaling ships hunting for the sperm whale. The sperm whale was hunted for its oil and blubber.

5

Whales must come to the surface to breathe.

Whales are **mammals**. Mammals give live birth to their young. Most mammals live on land, but whales live their entire lives in water.

Because they live in the ocean, many people think that whales are like fish. They are very unlike fish. Fish breathe through gills. Whales have lungs and breathe through **blowholes**. When whales come to the surface to breathe, water is seen shooting high into the air from the blowhole.

When whales come to the surface to breathe,
water is seen shooting high into the air from the blowhole.

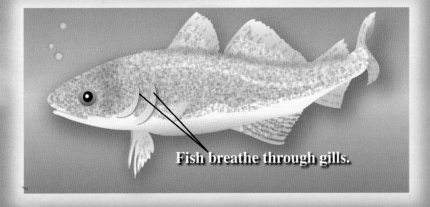

Fish breathe through gills.

Adult whale nursing a baby whale

Whales and fish are different in other ways. Fish have scales, but whales have hair like land mammals. Fish are cold-blooded animals, while whales are warm-blooded. Fish lay eggs, and the young fish hatch from the eggs. Whales give birth to live young. After birth, the young whales are nourished through milk from the mother's mammary glands. The young fish must find their own food.

A school of young fish feeding

Sperm whales were hunted
for their oil and blubber.

Today, many species of whales are
endangered. This means that they are few in
number. Because there are so few whales, they are
in danger of becoming extinct. The sperm whale
is an endangered whale. Sperm whales became

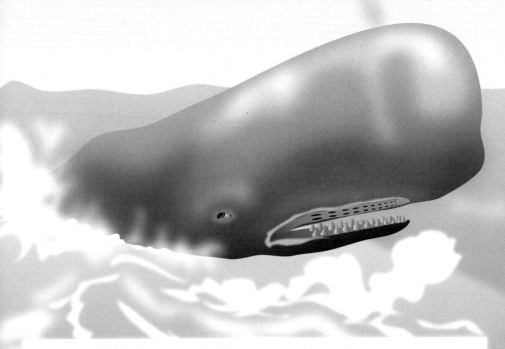

endangered because so many nations hunted them for meat and oil. Today, as an endangered whale, the sperm whale is protected. The efforts to protect them have led to an increase in the number of sperm whales.

Whales seem to be very playful. Sometimes, they jump high out of the water and slap the water with their tails as they come down. This makes a very loud noise. The slapping of the tail on the water is called **lobtailing**. Sometimes, a whale will seem to stand on its head and stick its tail out of the water. A whale may simply come to the surface and look around. Because whales are so playful, whale-watching is very enjoyable.

Slapping the tail on the water is called lobtailing.

You may know that birds **migrate**, but did you know that whales migrate too? Some whales migrate thousands of miles each year. Whales spend time in cold-water areas where they find

A pod of whales migrating

food. Then they migrate to warm-water areas
where they breed. They then migrate back to the
cold-water areas for food. Whales often migrate in
groups called **pods**.

All of the whales in a pod help watch over the baby whales. Mother whales often dive deep into the ocean for food. When they dive, the other whales watch over the baby whales. This watchful behavior ensures the safety of the baby whales. It is unlikely that a baby whale will become lost from the pod.

As you can see, whales are some of the largest and most interesting mammals on Earth.